Reflections on Surrender

Shannon Popkin & Janyre Tromp

credo
house publishers

Reflections on Surrender

Copyright © 2017 by Janyre Tromp and Shannon Popkin

All rights reserved.

Published in the United States by Credo House Publishers,
a division of Credo Communications, LLC, Grand Rapids, Michigan
www.credohousepublishers.com

ISBN-13: 978-1-625860-63-7

Printed in the United States of America

"God is in Control"

At church one morning, I (Shannon) started counting how many times I heard words about God being in control. "Well, I know I'm not in control of the timeline..." one mom told a group of us in the foyer, who all leaned in to hear the latest details about her adoption. We formed an impromptu prayer circle around her, and another woman prayed, "We trust that you are in control, God."

In the worship service, we sang, "In my heart and my soul, Lord I give you control..." And then as the pastor preached, he said, "God controls the seasons, the weather, the harvest..."

As the service progressed, I thought, "Yes, I believe this is true. God is in control." But we didn't even make it out of the church parking lot before I started behaving as though I was in control, not God.

It began with my son declaring from the back of the minivan that he didn't want to go to youth group that night, and my husband saying he was fine with that. I was not fine with it, and began listing my reasons to my husband, beside me in the driver's seat. He countered with his reasons, keeping his voice low so the kids wouldn't hear. But their bickering was so loud, *I* couldn't hear him either.

I whipped around, and made terse threats that were drastic enough to shut down the argument in the back seat (but not drastic enough to stop the shoving match that accompanied it).

What I Say Vs. How I Live

So basically, I spent the morning affirming that God was in control, then turned on my heel and began behaving like he wasn't. Like *I* had to take control and make things turn out right.

I find this is quite common, not just for me, but for other women, too. Because I write and speak on the topic of control, I've heard all kinds of Control Girl horror stories. We say that God is in control of our lives, but then we live like we are.

Rather than trusting, we fret. Rather than praying, we clamp down. Rather than hoping in God, we hope in ourselves to make everything turn out right.

And unfortunately when we do so, we create tension and misery, rather than the peace, joy, and security we envision.

So here's the question: How can we be faithfully following Jesus if we're making everyone miserable by trying to control them? Because that's not how Jesus lived. If we're following him, that's not how we should live either.

Jesus said, "Not my will but yours be done," then he turned on his heel and walked up a hill with a cross on his back. Jesus gave up control to God. He surrendered to the Father. He spent his life, not trying to control people, but pouring himself out as a sacrifice on their behalf.

So if I want to stop being a Control Girl and start being a Jesus Girl, I've got to do what Jesus did. I've got to let God direct my life, and spend myself in service of people, rather than trying to control them.

Easier said than done, but here's the key: Like with all behavior, our patterns of control are tied to our true beliefs. Not just what we say we believe, but what we truly believe. We act the way we act because we think the way we think. Transformation begins with our thought patterns.

Reminding Myself of What's True

That's where this book can help. It's filled with truth about control, ourselves, and God. The pages are filled with reminders that God is in control, and we aren't. These messages closely correlate with my book, *Control Girl: Lessons on Surrendering Your Burden of Control From 7 Women in the Bible*. While you don't have to work through that book to enjoy this one, we thought it would be fun to offer you the option.

The original artwork in this book was done by Janyre Tromp (who, by the way, was also the editor for my book, *Control Girl*). Our hope with this book is to entice you to make room for some white space in your life. As you add your color and design to the artwork, we hope you'll also soak your heart in the truth on the page. Look with fresh eyes at thoughts and ideas you might say you agree with, but perhaps don't live as though you believe. Consider the various angles, and savor the implications.

As you fill the pages of this book with color, fill your heart with its truth. Reflect on surrender, and ready your heart to say— as Jesus did, "Not my will but yours be done." (Luke 22:42)

A Control Girl's roots...

are planted in the soil of her own strength
She trusts in herself (not God)
to keep everything under control.

Like a doomed shrub in the desert,
she lives in parched, lonely places.

A Jesus Girl's roots...

are planted in the soil of God's Word.
She trusts in the Lord,
and refreshes her faith by reading His promises.

Like a green, fruit-laden tree beside a lake,
she is not fearful or anxious, even in extreme heat.

(from Jeremiah 17:5-8)

This
path of
surrender,
leads
to a place
where
God is in
Control,
and I am
free!

Do not be *Anxious* about your future, and all that you cannot *Control.*

Look at the birds. They have no way to produce a *Secure* future.

Yet God faithfully cares for them!

Surely then, you can trust that *God will care for you.*

(from Matthew 6:25-26)

faith is...

TRUSTING THAT
GOD IS *for* ME,
EVEN WHEN HE
KEEPS THINGS
from ME.

God gets the most glory,

not when he rips control from my hands,

But when I—

with open palms and hands lifted—

invite Him to take it.

"Not my will,
but
Yours
be done."
—Jesus
(Luke 22:42 NIV)

Envy
and
surrender
are opposite
responses.

Trust in the Lord with all your heart,

and do not lean on your own understanding of how to get or maintain control,

In all your ways, acknowledge God's Control over everything,

and He will make your paths straight.

(from Proverbs 3:5-6)

If I dwell in the uttermost parts of the sea, even there your hand will lead me and hold me.
from Psalm 139:7, 9

God never intended
for me to
carry the burden
of trying to
control everything.

Will I live in sweet surrender to God?

"The Lord is God...
... and there is no other."
Deuteronomy 4:35 NLT

Sweet Surrender

Lord, help me to walk by faith –
surrendering to your perspective,

Not by sight –
trying to control, based on how I see it.

(from 2 Corinthians 5:7)

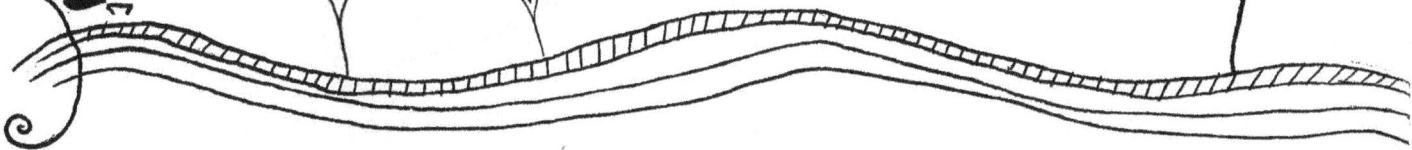

> Every day of my life
> was recorded in your book.
> Every moment was laid out
> before a single day had passed.
> (Psalm 139:16 NLT)

If God truly holds the future,
then I don't need to

worry,

If God's plot truly underlines
every part of my story,
then I don't need to

control;

Even when things go badly,
God's pen is still poised above
the details of my life, weaving together
a richly satisfying

happy ending.

Thank you...

...for joining us in reflecting on surrender. We're so thankful that you took the time to fill these pages with color, and fill your heart with truth about God and yourself.

As you close this book, we hope that you'll take with you the principles of relinquishing control. And if you do, we're guessing that you won't be the only one who will be influenced.

We each have a daughter who pushes us, encourages us, and inspires us. In fact, it was our daughters' encouragement to try new things (Shannon's daughter introduced her to adult coloring books and Janyre's daughter invited her to try zentangling), which led to putting this book together!

But as much as our daughters inspire us, we know how deeply we influence them. And we know it's the same for you. There are girls and women in your life who look to you for guidance as well.

Our hope is that as you take the path of surrender, you'll bring somebody– a daughter, a sister, or a friend–with you. Together, let's find the settled peace that only comes from releasing control to God. Let's inspire each other to surrender to God. Let's take steps, little by little, which transform us from Control Girls into Jesus Girls.

Sincerely,

Janyre & Shannon

About the Author & Artist

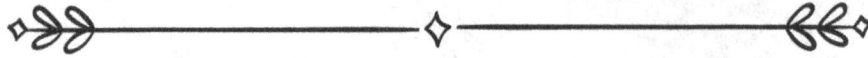

Janyre Tromp is an editor for Kregel Publications by day and a writer and artist by night. Unfortunately, she spilled coffee on her super cape and then the dryer ate it. So you'll just have to imagine that she can do it all!

Janyre blogs regularly on her own site as well as the Dove Parenting Blog. In addition to her current project (a full-length WWII novel), she has three traditionally published books: a juvenile fiction, *That Sinking Feeling,* and two board books in the *All About God's Animals* series.

Janyre first tried Zentangling alongside her daughter and was surprised to find she was actually good at it. Connect with Janyre at BeautifulUglyme.com, Twitter, Facebook, Instagram, or Pinterest.

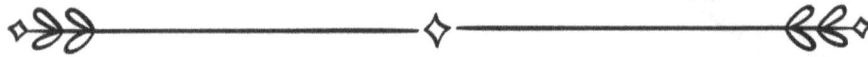

Janyre Tromp

Shannon Popkin is the author of *Control Girl: Lessons on Surrendering Your Burden of Control from Seven Women in the Bible.* As a speaker and writer, Shannon loves to blend her gifts for storytelling and humor with her passion for God's Word. Shannon is a contributing blogger at True woman.com.

Shannon is happy to have spent the past two decades married to Ken, who makes her laugh every day. Together, they live the fast paced life of parenting three teens. Connect with Shannon at shannonpopkin.com, Facebook, Twitter, Pinterest, or Instagram.

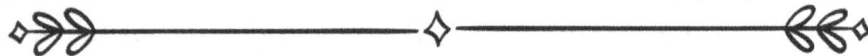

Shannon Popkin

Look for *Control Girl: Lessons on Surrendering Your Burden of Control from Seven Women in the Bible* wherever books are sold. Great for both individuals and small groups. Download a free discussion guide and meditation cards at shannonpopkin.com

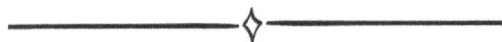

Thanks to Artisan Studio, MySunday.co, COB Studios, for allowing us to use their beautiful fonts.

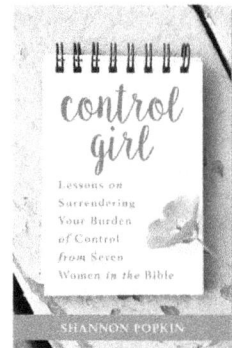

www.ingramcontent.com/pod-product-compliance
Lightning Source LLC
Chambersburg PA
CBHW081243020426
42331CB00013B/3287